SHOULD CHRISTIANS DRINK?

SHOULD CHRISTIANS DRINK?

The Case for
Total Abstinence

PETER MASTERS

THE WAKEMAN TRUST * LONDON

SHOULD CHRISTIANS DRINK?

© Peter Masters 1992
First published 1992

THE WAKEMAN TRUST
Elephant & Castle
London SE1 6SD

ISBN 1 870855 12 4

Cover design by Andrew Sides

Printed in Great Britain by J. W. Arrowsmith of Bristol

Contents

APPENDICES

Is Temperance a Law of Christ for Today?

F OR THE LAST 150 YEARS the overwhelming majority of Bible-believing Christians world-wide have been firmly committed to the practice of total abstention from alcohol. Only a relatively small proportion of evangelicals have demurred, reserving the right to drink in moderation. Now, however, the scene is changing, for with the general loosening of standards a surprising number of evangelicals are abandoning the long-held abstentionist view.

Interestingly, several books have recently appeared defending the 'right' of believers to drink in moderation. These all dismiss the majority position – the temperance position – with rather obvious contempt. Curiously, there appears to be little in print at the present time which presents the case for total abstention.

Here, then, are some of the reasons why those who love the Lord and seek to obey His Word should choose to turn away from alcoholic drinks.

In these pages the arguments in favour of temperance will be divided into two groups. There is one set of arguments used in support of the view that total abstention began in New Testament times. Although these arguments are, in the view of this writer, extremely powerful, it must be acknowledged that there is some basis for debate, and they will therefore be presented in the second part of the book.

However, there is another set of arguments which are even more important because they surely stand beyond all dispute and doubt. They are used in support of the following case: Regardless of whether abstention was required in New Testament times, it *became* the biblical duty of all Christians with the passing of time, as the size and character of the alcohol industry underwent dramatic change in terms of the quantity, potency and human costliness of its products. The biblical arguments in favour of this view seem so invincible that there is little room left for quibbling. For this reason we begin with this group of arguments, contending that, whatever may have been the case in Bible times, the *present-day Christian* is required by the principles taught in God's Word to stand entirely clear from the drinking of alcohol.

Part I

Good or Bad?
The Two Categories
of Human
Activity

1. Activities May Change Categories or 'Sides'

THERE IS NO DOUBT about the fact that wine was permitted to the Jews in Old Testament times. And *for the purposes of argument only* we will allow that wine may have been generally drunk by Christian believers in New Testament times. (Later we shall consider the arguments in support of the view that temperance began with the New Testament.) The question often asked is this: If wine was permitted to the 'church' of the Old Testament, and also to the first Christians, how can it be argued that present-day Christians should abstain as a matter of principle?

The first and most vital point to be understood is that the 'list' of forbidden or evil activities to be avoided by believers is not fixed or static throughout history. In general terms, we regard all activities as falling into one

11

of two categories – good activities or bad activities; righteous activities or unrighteous activities. But we must realise that it is possible for *some* activities to change from one category to the other depending on the circumstances. To give an obvious example, we may think of warfare. As far as the ancient Israelites were concerned their warfaring activities were not evil, because God had commanded them to fight. Their military actions were *God's own acts* of righteous judgement upon evil nations. However, many other acts of war, initiated by human beings, are evil. Indeed, they may be blatant mass murder.

Similarly, there is every justification for nations to defend themselves in war, and to take up arms to protect themselves, or for some essential international policing activity. There is such a thing as a 'just' war. However, there is also evil warfare, as in the case of aggressive, murderous invasion, motivated only by greed, malice or madness. Warfare may be justified or evil; it may change category according to the motives and circumstances.

Let us suppose we lived in a country which planned to invade a neighbouring state simply from a desire for conquest, or for the perverted delight of seeing people agonising under phosphor bombs. In these circumstances believers would surely have a duty to register as conscientious objectors. But suppose someone presented the following argument: 'Why ever should you regard this war as wrong in principle? Did not the

12

ancient Israelites go to war? If warfare was right in the Old Testament, is it not right for Christians today?'

Clearly such an argument would be foolish and mistaken, because it would fail to recognise that war is one of those activities which changes categories. It may be a just war or an evil war, according to the circumstances.

Sadly, however, this is precisely the kind of argument advanced by some Christians to support their use of alcohol. They point to *Deuteronomy 14.26*[*] saying, 'Because God allowed wine in those days it is clear that there is nothing wrong with it; Christians who abstain are therefore contradicting the Bible.'

We must never forget that *activities may change categories.* Even worldlings regard as unacceptable certain types of weapons and bombs which are expressly designed to maim and hurt. World-wide the cry goes up to ban chemical warfare with its horrific consequences in terms of pain and disfigurement. Working from the Old Testament we could argue that because the ancient Israelites were commanded to use weapons, there is no such thing as an evil weapon. But human weaponry has changed radically since those days.

---

[*]*And thou shalt bestow that money for whatsoever thy soul lusteth after, for oxen, or for sheep, or for wine, or for strong drink, or for whatsoever thy soul desireth: and thou shalt eat there before the Lord thy God, and thou shalt rejoice, thou, and thine household (Deuteronomy 14.26).*

13

Another example is to be seen in slavery. Slavery was never strictly intended for the Israelites of old, but it was permitted as an expedient. It was the lesser of two evils, the other being starvation. If people became bankrupt and unable to support their families, then a reasonably benevolent slavery at least provided for their needs. Accordingly, the Old Testament lays down certain rules for the proper treatment of Israelite slaves, forbidding their sale in a slave market, and providing for their release from slavery after six years. It also forbids bringing people into slavery by kidnap.

Because the Old Testament regulates the phenomenon of slavery, some Christians have argued (especially in the last century) that slavery cannot be regarded as evil. But we have seen how mankind exploited slavery so that it became one of the most hideous blots on human society. Few would now deny that slavery, as mostly practised by mankind, is a terrible evil. Things have moved on from the 'emergency social welfare' opportunity afforded by the modified form of slavery permitted to Israelites of old.

Yet another example of how activities may change from *good* (or tolerable) to *evil* is seen in the practice of *dancing*. The ancient Hebrew cultural dance was not intrinsically evil, but that does not mean that Christians should participate in dancing today. The modern dance is essentially a means of sensual and sexual arousal.

Because human activities may change in character

and therefore move from one category of acceptability to another, the New Testament does not give long, inflexible lists of activities which are approved, and activities which are disapproved. Instead we are given principles by which we judge all things *as they appear in our own age.* We must obviously ask whether activities are *morally* acceptable, conforming to the standards of the ten commandments, and all the other definitions of righteousness in the Bible. But what about activities which seem to be *morally* neutral, such as the eating of various foods and drinks?

The apostle Paul deals with this problem when he says, *All things are lawful unto me, but all things are not expedient: all things are lawful for me, but I will not be brought under the power of any (1 Corinthians 6.12).* Referring to activities (or possessions) which are not obviously immoral in character, the apostle lays down certain principles by which we may judge whether they are acceptable. Are they expedient (fitting, good, profitable), or will they have some mastery over us? A similar verse, *1 Corinthians 10.23,* adds the test – do they *edify,* that is, build us up or give positive benefits? Tests like these are given because activities which were relatively innocuous (or even non-existent) in the first century AD may become menacing and dangerous to Christian people in later times. The entire narcotics scene presents an obvious example of an industry which has emerged on a scale undreamed of in Bible times.

SHOULD CHRISTIANS DRINK?

The Christian abstainer's conviction is that alcoholic beverages have moved from the category of *beneficial* in Old Testament times, to the category of *grossly harmful and evil* in later centuries. Without any doubt the development of the liquor industry has unleashed a massive and cruel tidal wave of human tragedy and misery across the world. It has wrecked lives, homes, families, careers, even entire ethnic groups, causing more harm and heartache in human society than virtually anything else, with the possible exception of war.

We are speaking of a world-wide industry which now markets, so attractively and effectively, vast quantities of a powerful, psycho-active, mood-affecting, addictive drug, and we have to ask the prescribed biblical questions: Is it good, profitable, and positively beneficial, or is it unnecessary, harmful and enslaving? It is just not good enough to take refuge in what was permitted for the Israelites in a bygone culture. Just as we do with war, slavery and dancing, to mention only a few examples, we have to ask, Has wine changed? Has the wine industry changed? Has the use of wine changed? Have the dangers changed?

Alcohol – Our Favourite Drug, is the title of the report of a special committee of the Royal College of Psychiatrists. It asserts, 'Alcohol is the major public health issue of our time – overshadowing even that of tobacco, and dwarfing the problems of illicit drug abuse.' The compilers (eight doctors who are leaders in the field of alcohol abuse) insist that the damage caused by this 'potentially dangerous and addictive drug' is 'vastly greater than that caused by heroin addiction'.

Aside from addiction, official statistics show that alcohol is also the main factor in the deaths of 1,000 children every year in the UK, and of half the drivers who are killed under 25 years-of-age. It is heavily implicated in half of *all* recorded crimes, including half of all murders, half of all child-abuse cases, and half of all wife batterings. Such statistics as these give but a glimpse of the horrifying cruelties in which alcohol is involved, and again we must ask: Has there been some major change in its nature, availability and usage since the approval-in-moderation of Bible times?

In order to appreciate the great differences between the alcohol industry of Bible times and the industry of today we must be aware of some important features of wine-drinking in Israelite culture, as far as it affected ordinary people.

2. *Alcoholic Drinks of Bible Times were Weak*

THE COMMONLY AVAILABLE alcoholic drinks of Bible times were wines and beers, with wines prevailing in ancient Palestine. These were *considerably* weaker than many of the strong wines of today, particularly 'chaptalized' and fortified wines, not to mention distilled spirits, none of which existed in those days.

The highest achievable alcohol content of wines produced by ordinary fermentation – the only process available in Bible times – is around 14%. In those days, however, wine was not normally fermented anywhere near to that ceiling because of the unpleasant taste produced by extraneous bacteria which their technology could not eliminate. These joined in the fermentation process turning the sugar into vinegar. The common wines of Palestine were fermented for only three to four days (compared with the six-month period of the Greeks), and while their strength is not known, the indications are that they were extremely weak.

Andre Bustanoby, in his book, *The Wrath of Grapes*, writes against abstention and in favour of moderation only. But from a detailed examination of the ancient wine-making process he concludes that alcohol abuse was not a major problem to the ordinary people of ancient times because good-strength wine was expensive and not in great supply. The common wine, he asserts, was poor-quality wine of low alcohol content. Indeed, much of it never became true wine at all – 'It was just aerobically fermented must.'

'Must' is the juice of the grape, which begins to ferment as soon as it is pressed from the grape. The must was left in open jars or vats to undergo aerobic fermentation (in Palestine for only a few days). The next stage of the wine-making process – anaerobic fermentation (ie: shut off from air or oxygen) – was very difficult in olden times due to their porous containers and poor stoppers. Thus the cheaply produced 'ordinary' wines were stunted in development, sometimes lacking any anaerobic fermentation, which has been described as the 'birth' of the wine. Andre Bustanoby appropriately comments: 'Much of the confusion over the drinking habits of the ancients arises from a failure to understand this fact. Until the juice of the grape undergoes *anaerobic* fermentation it is really not wine. It is merely fermented must, or new wine of low alcohol content.'

The common wine of ancient Palestine was certainly fermented and no doubt intoxicating in quantity, but it was an exceptionally weak product by today's standards, estimated at being between 2% (for lightly fermented must) to 6% in strength.[*]

Some 1,200 years after the New Testament was written, human ingenuity discovered the process of alcohol distillation, ushering in a massive change in the potency and availability of alcoholic drinks. Yet 700 years further still along the road of history (and human misery) there are too many Christians who would like to pretend that none of this has happened. With the invention of distillation the top theoretical limit of 14% alcohol available in the very strongest wines immediately leapt. Nowadays, spirits of 40% (the normal bottled strength for gins, rums, brandies and whiskies) are commonplace. (Among the stronger spirits is the inappropriately named *Cana* of Majorca, bottled at 75%.)

The distillation process also led to the introduction of 'fortified' wines, which are strengthened by the addition of distilled alcohol. (Examples are sherry, madeira and port, ranging from 16 to 20% alcohol.) In addition, even many 'ordinary' wines these days boast an alcohol

---

[*] See Appendix 1 on *The Wine Words of the Old Testament* for information on the *strong drink* of the *Authorised Version*.

content 5% higher than earlier products due to the use of the 'chaptalization' process (discovered by one of Napoleon's ministers of state).

Clearly, the unsophisticated technology of ancient times pegged down the usable alcohol content of the wines, and even where taste was sacrificed for strength, 14% was always nature's limit, for once that strength is achieved in the fermentation process, the yeast cells die.*

The poorest people throughout the Mediterranean and the Near East often had to contend with very low quality, weak wine made from the residue of the crushed grapes, cooked with water and then mixed with some fermenting grapes to give it life.

Even the low (2%–6%) strength of ordinary wine, however, is not the whole picture, for it is most probable that the Jews of old, like other peoples of those times, drank their wine in a diluted form, rather like a cordial. It is well attested that in the cultures both of the Greeks and the Romans, wine – weak as it was by comparison with many of today's drinks – was usually mixed with water. Sometimes the degree of dilution was very great.

---

*It is true that Pliny (AD 62–113), the Roman statesman and orator, made mention of a wine so strong that it could burn, but as this would require an alcohol content of 30% (unachievable before the discovery of distillation) and as such a feat is nowhere else attested, it is best to regard the claim as being colourful.

Homer's *Odyssey* includes mention of a 20-to-1 water-wine mixture in the case of a strong wine – and we remember that *strong* in those days could not exceed 14%.

The Greeks regarded anyone who drank undiluted wine as a barbarian! And in the terminology of the Western Mediterranean the very word for wine indicated a watered-down serving. A neat drink had to be especially described as being 'unmixed'.

Did the Jews also water down their wine? There is powerful evidence that they followed the same practice as others in this respect. Certainly by Roman times the Rabbinical writings of the Jews mention the mixing of water with wine for the observing of Jewish feasts. The Jewish *Mishna* says that four cups of wine were poured out for the Passover, water being mixed with it because it was considered too strong to be drunk alone. The Jewish literature refers to two or even three parts of water to one of wine. The term for this diluted wine was *mazug*.

Are there any indications of this in the Bible? Yes indeed, for in *Song of Solomon 5.1* we read of the wine being mixed with milk, perhaps a special luxury by way of an alternative to water. The same luxury may be the sense of *Isaiah 55.1*: *Come, buy wine and milk without money and without price. Proverbs 9.2* and *5* may describe the practice of mixing the wine with water or milk: *She hath mingled her wine . . . Come, eat of my bread, and drink of the wine which I have mingled.* The banquet of instruction is ready, for the beasts are slaughtered, the table is spread, and the wine freshly mixed – indicating the immediate readiness of the feast. While it is possible that this was a mingling of wine and spices, this is unlikely in view of the fact that there is a special Hebrew term to describe *spiced* wine (which is used in *Song of Solomon 8.2*). The language of *Proverbs 9* perfectly suits the practice (described by the Greeks) of mingling the wine in a large bowl immediately before serving. (The Greeks called this bowl a *krater.*)

Yet another reference to mixed wine is in *Proverbs 23.29-30: Who hath redness of eyes? They that tarry long at the wine; they that go to seek mixed wine.* Keil and Delitzsch (after Hitzig and also Fleischer) take the view that this refers to people who 'searched' or 'tested' the strength of the mixture of wine and water (presumably in the wine-house). They did this because a high alcohol content was important to them, as intoxication was their goal. These great Hebraists quoted are certain that a wine-water mix is in mind here.

In the New Testament there is a verse which strongly implies that wine was taken in diluted form. This verse, *Revelation 14.10,* goes out of its way to specify an *undiluted* wine as an appropriate symbol for the wrath of God. Speaking of any person who worships and obeys the beast, the verse reads: *The same shall drink of the wine of the wrath of God, which is poured out* WITHOUT

24

MIXTURE *into the cup of his indignation.*[*] The meaning is that in hell God's wrath will be undiluted – untempered by mercy and grace.

Setting such references in the context of the widespread practice of the ancient world it is most probable that the wine of the Israelites, although very weak, was normally taken in diluted form.[‡] (Whoever heard of watered-down wine in our day?) The intended provision was a pleasant and 'sanitary' drink, helpful in an age and climate full of biological dangers.

This writer agrees with the scholarly conclusion of the *International Standard Bible Encyclopædia* (Vol 5, page 3087) that the wine of the ancients was mixed with water as well as with spices.

It is also important to recognise that the 'wine' words of both Old and New Testaments may also extend to a non-alcoholic beverage derived from fermented wine. Across the ancient world a cordial was often made by the process of boiling wine (the alcohol quickly evaporating away) and then diluting the resulting sticky syrup with water. As long as it was drunk immediately this would be free from alcohol. Such a drink is referred to in Egyptian, Roman and Jewish literature. The Jews referred to it as *yayin mebushal.*

---

[*] See Appendix 2 on *The Mixed Wine of Isaiah 1.22.*

[‡] This verse also proves conclusively that the Bible writers used the word *mixture* to mean *water* as well as (in some cases) herbs and spices.

3. The Social Framework of Israelites was Strict toward Alcohol

THIRDLY, WE MUST TAKE NOTE of the *social framework* within which this sanitary alcoholic beverage was permitted. It was a framework in which drunkenness was abhorred, and in which kings and princes were commanded (in the Scriptures) to be abstainers, partly because of their high responsibilities, and doubtless also to provide an example of sobriety *(Proverbs 31.4-5).** The priests also were forbidden strong drink (on pain of death) when officiating in the

---

It is not for kings, O Lemuel, it is not for kings to drink wine; nor for princes strong drink: lest they drink, and forget the law, and pervert the judgment of any of the afflicted (Proverbs 31.4-5).

tabernacle and when ministering to the people *(Leviticus 10.9-10)*.*

Proverbs 31.6-7‡ prescribed strong drink as an appropriate medicinal aid to relieve those dying in agony, and also to suppress the mental torment of those suffering from suicidal depression. However, the manner in which these recommendations were made clearly shows that mood-affecting levels of alcohol were not approved of for society in general. People were to be content with a weaker or diluted beverage.

When we consider the 'woes' pronounced in *Isaiah 5* upon those who are *mighty to drink wine*, we get a clear picture of the immense official, prophetic disapproval which surrounded excessive drinking among the Israelites. And nothing could be plainer than the emphatic command of *Proverbs 23.20, Be not among winebibbers*, which is plainly an absolute prohibition from going into drinking places, and also (the verse goes on to say) from attending feasts or banquets where drinking and gluttony were the chief attractions.

Do not drink wine nor strong drink, thou, nor thy sons with thee, when ye go into the tabernacle of the congregation, lest ye die: it shall be a statute for ever throughout your generations: and that ye may put difference between holy and unholy, and between unclean and clean (Leviticus 10.9-10).

‡*Give strong drink unto him that is ready to perish, and wine unto those that be of heavy hearts. Let him drink, and forget his poverty, and remember his misery no more (Proverbs 31.6-7).*

SOCIAL FRAMEWORK WAS STRICT

How different is all this from our culture today! Times have totally changed. Values have certainly become reversed. Heavy social drinking is now wholly justified and approved. The most admired people – the role models – drink heavily. Professional people, media people and 'opinion-formers' such as politicians, are recognised to be among the heaviest drinkers in society. The absence of any stigma on drinking is seen from the extent to which alcohol is flaunted at all social celebrations and occasions at all levels of society. According to general public perception, today it is the feeble person, or the anti-social, miserable person, or the peculiar person who fails to make effective use of the psycho-active and mood-affecting properties of alcohol.

Short of killing someone while drunk at the wheel of a car, heavy drinking is no longer an offence to society. Far from being discouraged, it is urged and stimulated by a colossal advertising budget of more than two hundred million pounds every year in the UK alone. So successful is this unrelenting campaign, that the national expenditure on alcoholic drinks adds up to more than half the total spending on food. Can anyone deny that there is a gigantic difference between the attitude of the biblical Jews towards alcohol, and the attitude of our present society?

4. Supplies of Wine were Limited in Bible Times

FOURTHLY, IT MUST BE appreciated that wine was not particularly plentiful in ancient times. There was no big wine industry in Israel comparable with later world developments. For the most part the making of wine was a cottage industry. Some years ago an article appeared in a Christian magazine which gave the following information about the marriage feast at Cana, at which the Lord turned the water into wine. It was noted that six 30-gallon* pots would have yielded 1,440 pints of wine. This, said the article, if shared out between 200 people would have given them seven pints each – a great deal to drink for a single day!

Of course, the writer had his figures all wrong. The

---

*John 2.6 – a firkin is equal to ten gallons.

fact is that a wedding feast of the Jews in those days would have lasted at least a week, and possibly longer. Also, a figure of 400 guests would be *much* more likely than 200, given the custom of the times. These adjustments would reduce the daily ration of wine to half a pint per person per day. In these circumstances, the half-pint would have needed considerable dilution (*at least* six parts water to one of wine) to provide an adequate intake of fluid for each day. Thus the wine which began at a strength of, say, 2–6% of alcohol, could well have been weakened to ½–1%. This is, of course, guesswork, but Cana certainly provides no basis for the notion of a society which drank strong wine heavily. (In the less likely event of a much smaller and shorter wedding feast, it is possible that the Lord may have made the wine in a diluted state, ready to serve.)

The most significant point in the record, however, is the fact that the people of Cana ran out of wine so quickly. They evidently could not send to the next village to make up the shortfall (presumably because they were equally short of wine), nor could they scavenge the town off-licences! The fact is that a cottage industry simply could not cope with one too many weddings. Wine was not that plentiful. The wedding at Cana occurred in mid-March, four months before the next grape harvest. They were only two-thirds of the way through the year and the town had run out of wine. This would suggest that what they supplied at the beginning of the wedding was the stand-by material with an inferior taste (possibly boiled-down to syrup for preservation, and later diluted and re-fermented).

The data supplied in *John 2* thus draws attention to the relatively modest production of wine by the local-ised cottage industry of the day. The wealthy, perhaps, could be sure of a good supply, and the inveterate drunkard may have been able to hoard what he wanted, but for most village communities there was simply not enough wine to support a society of heavy drinkers.

Once again we are bound to compare the situation of those days with what emerged with the passing of cent-uries. The modest cottage industry, restricted to the natural process of fermentation, eventually became the massive alcohol industry of the present day – greatly changed by the invention of the distillation process, and by numerous advances in the selection and manage-ment of yeast strains used in the fermentation process, not to mention alcohol-boosting techniques such as Napoleonic chaptalization.

Vast breweries, wineries and distilleries now straddle the world, producing quantities of beers, wines and spirits simply undreamed of in Bible times. Who has not heard of the wine lake of the EC? The alcohol industry stands ready and able to increase yet further the thirst, consumption and dependence of a vulnerable world.

How plentiful is alcohol today? Britons pay over 22 billion pounds every year for their enormous quantities, and seven million adults exceed the recommended safe weekly limits of consumption, according to a UK Government paper.*

Some 80,000 pubs, 35,000 licensed clubs, and 48,000 off-licences unite to supply the ongoing thirst of the land – 163,000 outlets not counting the multitude of high street supermarkets.

Professor Alan Maynard of the Department of Health Economics at York University has calculated that the total *true* cost of Britain's drinking, taking account of alcohol-caused sickness absence, unemployment, health costs, police and court costs is an astounding £2,000,000,000 every year. 28,000 people die prematurely with alcohol-related illnesses, and up to a million people suffer serious harm, socially or physically, because of alcohol misuse.

Times have changed, and we are certainly not now living in the cultural environment of the Bible. An understatement is inevitable and unavoidable – the alcohol industry is not the same!

---

*The *Lord President's Report on Action Against Alcohol Misuse, 1991*

5. Which Category is Wine Now In?

W E MAY LOOK BACK at the cottage industry of Bible times as producing a wine hardly comparable with that of later history. The ordinary beverage, often no more than low-alcohol must, and not rising above 6% strength, was most probably taken weak or diluted, in line with the practice of the Mediterranean region in those times. It was often necessary for reasons of gastric hygiene. It was consumed within a Jewish social framework which abhorred strong drink and drunkenness, and which required nobles and on-duty priests to abstain. It was in limited supply so far as ordinary people were concerned. We could add that the wine of those days was certainly not produced in the enormous range of flavours and types, so attractive to the human palate, that we see today. For the very wealthiest of her citizens, first-century Rome boasted 75 varieties (some laced with such substances as gypsum, resin, pitch and even sea-water), but for the masses, and especially in less-sophisticated Palestine, the range of wines was pathetically limited.

The liquor industry now markets a huge variety of distinctive and subtle flavours, many being highly intoxicating. Alcohol is no longer necessary as a sanitary drink, nor is it any longer in scarce supply. It is as plentiful and available as anyone could possibly wish, and it is heavily promoted within a society which has long since abandoned all taboos.

The relatively safe beverage of ancient times has changed so greatly that the biblical questions (pre-scribed by *1 Corinthians 6.12* and *10.23*) must obviously be levelled once again at the alcohol issue: is it expedient, good, profitable and beneficial, or is it much too capable of mastering or enslaving the one who indulges? Does drink, with its associations, now come into the category of the *unfruitful works of darkness* with which the Christian should have *no fellowship*?

The answers to these questions are not hard to determine. Fermented wines and other alcoholic drinks have surely crossed from the category of beneficial to the category of unnecessary – indeed, into the category of substances which are cruelly and insidiously harmful. Without doubt, alcohol has become a chief tool of Satan to inflict misery and ruin upon this sin-sick world. We are compelled to ask, What business can a Christian have in subscribing to the consequences of such an industry?

We have already referred to the invention of the distillation process some 700 years ago, marking a new era of chemical abuse for the human race. Can anyone deny the alcohol revolution since Bible times? Can anyone explain away the world-wide evidence – a veritable mountain of misery – proving that a monumental change has taken place in the production and the effects of alcohol? Can anyone seriously refute the degree to which alcohol is now the inspiration and strength behind the most horrific crimes committed by human beings? The New Testament calls us to *prove all things,* to *hold fast that which is good,* and to *abstain from all appearance of evil (1 Thessalonians 5.21-22).* Everything that we do must be tested and approved – including things which in the context of Old Testament times possessed a more wholesome character and purpose.

We do not, of course, suggest that there was no drunkenness in ancient Israel! Alcohol has always held danger, and it has always been drunk to excess, producing much misery. But we are forced to recognise the dramatic shift from the *relatively* innocuous, sanitary (and therefore beneficial) everyday beverage of ancient Palestine, to the highly potent, and aggressively marketed drinks now manufactured in vast quantities. Without doubt alcohol has become a mighty force in society, stimulating crime, inflaming passions, wrecking lives, encouraging unbelievable heartlessness and cruelty, and claiming millions to the bondage of addiction.

6. Texts Which Demand a Response

I N THE LIGHT OF all these observations we must look very seriously at the large family of Bible passages which tell us how believers must respond to things which are inextricably connected with sinful enticement, bondage, cruelty, or the ethos and lifestyle of this present world-system. The strongest arguments for total abstention on the part of Christian believers are based on these texts.

Ephesians 5.8 is an example. Paul declares, *For ye were sometimes darkness, but now are ye light in the Lord: walk as children of light.* Then (in verse 11) he says, *And have no fellowship* [no interaction whatsoever] *with the unfruitful works of darkness, but rather reprove them.*

It is true that the apostle primarily has in view the orgies of sex and idolatry prevalent in the society of that time but he nevertheless states a principle which we must apply in our day to everything which promotes or assists sinfulness. And is not alcohol nowadays the elixir of life to a godless society?

In *Romans 1.29-31* the apostle provides a long list of evil deeds, but there is one phrase – *inventors of evil things* – which is of particular relevance to the alcohol question. In this phrase, *evil* literally means *worthless*, or *evil in character*. It is a characteristic of this fallen world that worldly minds invent evil, worthless things which undermine moral values, de-stabilising good conduct and character.

In the 1990s the advertising of alcohol has become so audacious as to flood the street hoardings with posters promoting spirits to the young as the vital catalyst for sexual adventure and indulgence. Films, television 'soaps' and novels have, of course, been doing this for years, and the mighty liquor industry has become, beyond all doubt, an enemy of the rational, intelligent use of the mind, and a powerful tool and promoter of moral destruction. It stands as a worthless contrivance of this world, which (by the standard of *Romans 1*) is under the condemnation of God.

In *Romans 12.9* we find another Greek word for *evil*. Paul says, *Abhor that which is evil; cleave to that which is good.* The word *abhor* means *shudder away from,* while the word *evil* here means *damaging* or *harmful.* This word does not describe the *character* of a thing, but its

40

effect. Something may, strictly speaking, be morally acceptable (or morally 'neutral'), but if it has harmful, damaging consequences, then it is evil in its effect. Here Paul commands us to shudder away from things which only (or chiefly) do harm.

We should shudder that the world has taken alcohol and made it such a force for destruction, misery and horror.

We should shudder at the way it subdues the higher senses even of the countless men and women who drink only moderately.

We should shudder away from a product which causes an estimated 10 to 16 million children under eighteen in the USA to have to grow up in the living nightmare of a shattered, alcoholic home. With a record such as this, what is the difference in harmfulness between alcoholic beverages and hard drugs?

We should shudder that the greatest component of the human frame – the rational faculty – is regularly blurred and distorted by alcohol, so that the baser part (the animal part) of human nature is released. This is, of course, the very effect which people so often want to bring about – even some Christians. They *want* the mind, the seat of their anxieties, to be dulled! They *want* the lower instincts to be free. They *want* their feelings to be affected, and their cares to be slightly anaesthetised. That is the whole idea. But it is a harmful effect: a drug is being directed against God's highest gift, the *reason.*

41

Paul's command could not possibly be more relevant: 'Shudder away from that which is harmful and injurious.'

We have to ask, What has happened to alcohol since Bible times? What has happened to the industry? What is it that is pressed upon everyone today? Is it the original weak (and probably watered-down) product of a small-scale cottage industry as in Bible times, or is it something altogether different? What category is the activity of drinking alcohol now to be placed in – good or bad? How should we look at it in the light of the texts which govern our approach to these things?

In *1 Thessalonians 5.22*, as we have already noted, Paul commands, *Abstain from all appearance of evil.* Here the Greek translated *evil* again means *harmful* or *damaging.* Every injurious, cruel, and spoiling attitude or activity is to be abstained from. What category is alcohol now in? Is it evil or harmful? Is it not something which has degenerated from its original virtue?

In *1 Corinthians 10.6* Paul applies another principle, drawing a lesson from the experience of the children of Israel in their wilderness wanderings. He says, *Now these things were our examples, to the intent we should not lust after EVIL things.* Here the Greek word for *evil* is, *worthless,* or *evil in character.* We should not lust after worthless things, says Paul, *as they also lusted.* This is a reference to the lusting in the wilderness recorded in *Numbers 11.4-6,* when the children of Israel suddenly began to lust after the food of the Egyptians.

We read in *Numbers*: *And the mixt multitude that was among them fell a lusting: and the children of Israel also wept again, and said, Who shall give us flesh to eat? We remember the fish, which we did eat in Egypt freely; the cucumbers, and the melons, and the leeks, and the onions, and the garlick: but now our soul is dried away: there is nothing at all, beside this manna, before our eyes.*

On the surface, it is rather surprising that longing for meat, fish and vegetables should be such an evil thing to do. It is very strange that Paul should call foods such as leeks, onions, melons and cucumbers *evil*.

How is it that such foodstuffs were evil for the Jews in the wilderness, whereas the Bible permits them at other times? The answer is that these things *were* evil at that time because in order to get them the children of Israel would have had to go back to the society of Egypt. While they were in the wilderness they were being fed by the Lord in a miraculous way. But to long for the foods of their former life in bondage was highly offensive to God because it showed an amazing ingratitude for the manna, and it involved a strong yearning to be back in Egypt. (This is a classic case of how something quite innocent may become an evil thing in certain circumstances.)

All this may be applied to the Christian and alcohol. There are many activities which are not intrinsically evil, but they become worthless and evil to believers if they find so little attraction in the blessings of the Christian life that we *must* have the produce of 'Egypt' (the delights and comforts of our former, unconverted lives), then we greatly insult the Lord, and commit the sin of base ingratitude. These verses must speak to us, and direct our consciences.

Is *today's* alcohol cult acceptable to God? Which side is it on – the Lord's side, or the devil's? Has it not become a principal instrument of Satan to ensnare souls and keep them from the kingdom of God? Are there not millions of people so attached to their tipple that they dare not allow themselves to be drawn under the sound of the Gospel? They instinctively *know* that the things they depend upon would have to be surrendered if they came to seek the things of God. They seem to know this better than some Christians!

If the alcohol industry has become firmly identified with the interests of God's arch-enemy, then we should have no relationship with it on the basis of the commands represented in these verses of Scripture. To remain distinct and separate from the tools and weapons of Satan is vital to our calling and testimony.

In *Ephesians 4.27* Paul puts it this way: *Neither give place to the devil.* If something is an instrument of Satan, and is obviously powerfully used by him in the lives of millions of people, then we are not to give place to it for a moment.

Jude 23 can equally be applied to the alcohol issue. We

are to hate *even the garment spotted by the flesh*. The believer is not meant to have even a toe, let alone a foot, in the lifestyle of this world, nor to imbibe its major tonic; its essential elixir of life and well-being.

Other texts insist that we must never put ourselves in the way of temptation, or render ourselves vulnerable to sin. An example of such texts is *Romans 13.14* where we are told, *Make not provision for the flesh.* This is a command of God! Therefore, if alcoholic beverages have changed, so that people no longer dilute the wine, but approve and drink stronger and more potent products, then we should abstain.

A single glass of a typical fortified wine (such as sherry) contains 16–20% of alcohol, a percentage very rapidly absorbed by the body to give a pronounced effect as a depressant, sedative and tranquillizer.

Just one glass begins to suppress the body's mechanisms for the control of urges and inhibitions, making the person feel pleasantly calm, a little liberated, and more talkative. By the second glass the depression of the brain and nervous system is well under way, mood and judgement being measurably affected. But the child of God is absolutely forbidden by *Romans 13.14* from pandering to fleshly desires, in this case, the 'effect' of modern alcoholic drinks.

We return to two passages already referred to, *1 Corinthians 6.12* and *10.23*, and set out the questions which arise. A*ll things are lawful unto me*, says Paul, *but* *all things are not expedient … I will not be brought under the power of any … all things edify not.*

Are alcoholic drinks expedient (fitting, appropriate) for the testimony of a believer in the light of all the changes which have taken place, and the role which alcohol now plays in society? Will alcoholic drinks (remembering their great potency in modern times) bring me under their power to any degree?

Do alcoholic drinks edify? Do they impart any benefit, as the pleasant sanitary drinks of olden times did? Or do they now take anything from those who drink, placing believers at risk, blunting their testimony, and causing them to support, encourage and condone an evil industry?

And while looking at the 'tests' laid down by the apostle Paul to be applied to all our thoughts, intentions, plans and activities, how do modern alcoholic drinks stand up in the light of *Philippians 4.8 – Whatsoever things are honest,* and so on?

Are today's strongly intoxicating alcoholic drinks *honest,* or are they the tools of unreality and mood-engineering? Are they *just,* or do they tamper with mental judgement and discernment? Are they *pure,* or do they (in the least degree) inflame and arouse fallen passions? Are they *lovely* (ie: love-communicating), or are they selfish, and in large quantities quarrelsome and violent?

Are they of *good report,* or do they have a bad

reputation in the areas of moral conduct, intelligent thought, and human kindness? Is there *any virtue* or *praise*, or is there (taste considerations aside) none at all?

These are just some of the passages, typical of many, which have been referred to for years in support of Christians abstaining from alcohol.

We have a duty to distance ourselves from Satan's agencies for the undermining of rational control and moral behaviour. Similarly, we must have nothing to do with Satan's means of inflicting failure, tragedy and distress on literally millions of people world-wide. Alcohol has become such an agency. It is alluring; it is destructive; it secures a great hold on the minds of people; it is addictive, and it is one of the tempter's main safeguards against the call of the Gospel. Furthermore, it gives him access to the minds and bodies even of believers, if they yield to it.

It was the burden of involvement with alcoholic misery which in 1867 moved twenty-year-old Fred Charrington, just converted, to renounce his huge private income and millionaire future as heir to a brewery fortune. He was on his way one evening to teach a class of illiterate boys in a London East End slum. Passing a public house called 'The Rising Sun' he saw a poor, raggedly-clothed woman with two little children clutching on to her skirt, crying with hunger. The woman went to the pub door and called out for her husband. Suddenly, the man rushed out and battered the pathetic trio to the ground.

As he looked on, appalled, Charrington's eyes caught sight of his own family name emblazoned across the door of the pub. His mind responded immediately. 'You have knocked your wife down,' he said to himself, 'and with the same blow you have knocked me out of the brewery business.' For the remaining sixty-eight years of his life, Fred Charrington was probably the best-known temperance campaigner of the period, his youthful decision representing the only possible heart-response to the commands of the New Testament.

There are two sorts of Christian who appear to ignore texts such as those examined here. There are those who have no light on the subject. They have simply never thought about it. Perhaps they come from a background where professing Christians imbibe alcohol without any inhibition of conscience, and this has dulled their own instinctive awareness that alcoholic beverages are to be regarded with great suspicion.

Sadly, however, there is a second kind of Christian. These friends know the temperance arguments well, and they are familiar with the texts, but they simply do not wish to consider the issue. They say, 'No, I am not willing to question the rightness of drinking alcohol.' Their response is as blunt and as indifferent as that.

As Christian people we are trusted by the Lord. He has given us rules to apply, and we are trusted to apply them. We must carefully weigh whether or not a particular activity or substance is currently evil or worldly, either in essence or in effect. But the fact that we are trusted to exercise discernment does not mean that it is *optional* to apply God's standards. They are absolutely authoritative over us.

There have always been believers who, though aware of the biblical arguments for abstention, are content to remain weak in the faith, never taking any kind of personal stand. This is particularly grievous when one considers how relatively easy it is for a Christian to abstain. Assuming that a person is not suffering from alcoholic addiction, there are not many things as easy to give up as alcoholic drinks! If believers can see the principles, and yet cannot take a firm line on this matter, then they are unlikely to take a stand on anything! Such friends train their souls to be weak on everything. If we cannot separate from the ungodliness of today's alcohol industry, what will we separate from? The answer is, probably nothing!

We are a distinct people and we are called to be separate from the world. The apostle Peter extols the distinctiveness of believers in *1 Peter 2.9*: *But ye are a chosen generation, a royal priesthood, an holy nation, a peculiar people* [ie: a people for God's own possession]; *that ye should shew forth the praises of him who hath called you out of darkness into his marvellous light.* Our testimony depends on our distinctiveness.

Alcohol is an essential part of a pleasure-worshipping

society. It is Satan's fermented river of false hope, false consolation, false happiness, and false courage. It is his way of binding millions to this world; and it is one of the chief symbols of this world's apostate culture. With our whole testimony at stake, we note the appeal of Peter that believers should walk – *having your conversation honest among the Gentiles: that, whereas they speak against you as evildoers, they may by your good works, which they shall behold, glorify God in the day of visitation (1 Peter 2.12).*

Because alcohol is now so intrinsically worldly, an abstainer is immediately marked out. A believer may 'put in a word' for the Lord here and there for years without making much impression, but the moment a drink is refused, that believer is noticed at once, and never forgotten. There is no finer way of being seen to be distinct than to take a stand on these things.

To be known in the office as an abstainer is a fine way of 'breaking the ice' for witness, and countless believers have found that this has led to many fruitful and blessed conversations with unconverted colleagues.

We want no part of Satan's river of delusion and heartache, and we have no need for it either. Of course, the Christian must never come across as pompous or 'holier-than-thou'. By the grace of God we have to learn to express ourselves in a humble and winning way. No matter *how* we may decline a drink, the world may still *speak against you as evildoers.* Nonetheless, we must hold the line, so that *they may by your good works, which they shall behold, glorify God in the day of visitation.*

In this consideration of texts we have not touched upon the Christian duty of responsible stewardship (a most important topic in connection with the great expense of modern alcoholic drinks in many countries). Nor have we considered texts covering the *example* of believers to the young and to other vulnerable people in a society which encourages intoxicants. This issue is raised in later chapters. Nevertheless, such texts as we have referred to demand a response from all sincere believers who want to walk before the Lord in obedience to His will.

Part II

Abstinence in the New Testament

A Gradual
Introduction

HAVING PRESENTED arguments to show that the alcoholic drink industry has moved into the category of 'evil things' with which Christians should have nothing to do, we now come to an entirely different set of arguments which seek to show that abstinence actually began in New Testament times. These arguments are both venerable and powerful, and Christian writers who oppose abstinence make no attempt to answer most of them. Yet we do not claim that *all* these arguments are absolutely conclusive. That is why the 'abhor evil things' case has been presented first, because that case is surely incontrovertible. Nevertheless, the evidence that abstinence began in the New Testament demands the closest attention.

By way of background, we accept that wine was

certainly sanctioned for the Israelites in Old Testament times as an everyday sanitary drink. From the evidence already referred to we believe that it was a relatively weak product, and was most probably watered down like a cordial, and perhaps often boiled prior to dilution (thus losing any intoxicating properties). There was clearly great preservative value in the fermented wine of those days, long before the evils of a mass production alcohol industry emerged.

We also remember that the Israelites of old were a 'mixed multitude' of saints and sinners together, and there was therefore greater latitude in their laws than in the standards of conduct later prescribed for the wholly regenerate membership of New Testament churches. In olden times, for example, divorce was allowed because of the hardness of their hearts. Likewise polygamy, though never sanctioned, was at times tolerated.

In the New Testament, standards advanced, and we have many firm exhortations to separate from activities which are injurious, and which are part and parcel of a godless world. Among these exhortations, as we shall show, are those which call us to turn away from intoxicants.

Of course, the new standard on alcohol was brought in gently and gradually in the New Testament for the simple reason that vast numbers of early Christians were converted Jews who were accustomed to the consumption of weak wine as permitted under the old order. Nevertheless, we believe that principles were laid down in the New Testament which would prepare Christians for the different alcohol-culture of non-Jewish nations (where drunkenness was rife), and for the future emergence of a mass production alcohol industry. However, as alcohol did not become intrinsically evil overnight, the new standard was not imposed with total and immediate insistence.

A parallel is seen in the latitude over the keeping of the Sabbath in New Testament times. Many converted Jews continued to keep the Jewish Sabbath as well as the Lord's Day. They had always kept the Sabbath, and they felt acutely uncomfortable about not doing so. Other aspects of the law also continued to be observed by converted Jews. The response of the apostles was very gentle and accommodating to the Jewish conscience. As long as the people concerned did not think that their Sabbath observance contributed in any way to their salvation, their observance of it was for a time allowed and overlooked.

The Jews were given time to recover from the discomfort of abandoning all their former practices. Said Paul, *Him that is weak in the faith receive ye (Romans 14.1)*, and he was speaking about converted Jews who still followed the Jewish food laws to the letter. He talked about those who had a *weak conscience (1 Corinthians 8.12)*. All this helps us to see why the New Testament did not bring in an immediate absolute prohibition of all alcoholic beverages.

There were very many Jews, now converted, who had strictly followed the permission of God to make wine and drink it in moderation. Why should it be declared instantly wicked? The great evil of alcohol in the world was not yet fully apparent, and there was still a health benefit in the availability of a sanitary drink.

The new standard of abstinence, therefore, came in as a voluntary response to the understanding of New Testament light, and not as an immediately and universally enforced rule. This explains why there are passages in the New Testament which indicate that some church members still drank wine. Moderation was enforced, while abstention was only announced and 'called for'. The people were given time in all these things. Nevertheless, as we shall now show, abstention was implicit in New Testament teaching, and doubtless many believers saw that light, and gladly obeyed.

1. We are a Kingdom of Priests

OUR FIRST ARGUMENT for the view that abstinence began in the New Testament was advanced by our temperance forebears long ago. It focuses on God's requirement that Old Testament kings, and also priests on Temple duty, should abstain from alcohol. Sadly, many Christians nowadays are inclined to be amused at this argument, and to dismiss it rather lightly. They find it far-fetched. But this is only a symptom of the fact that the deeply spiritual themes of the Bible, not to mention the significance of *types*, are not properly appreciated in this rationalistic, clinical age – not even among sound, solidly reformed believers.

The argument runs thus:– In *Leviticus 10.8-11* the Lord absolutely prohibited the drinking of alcohol by the priests while engaged in tabernacle (later Temple) duties, or while teaching the statutes of the Lord.* The passage about kings and princes not drinking appears in the words taught to King Lemuel by his mother *(Proverbs 31.4-6)*.‡ *Lemuel* means *belonging to God,* and is generally thought to be a symbolic name for Solomon. If this is correct, then the divine standard had obviously been revealed to David, the first *godly* king.

The ongoing significance of the alcohol prohibition for on-duty priests and Levites, as well as for kings and princes, should be obvious. We who are Christian believers have been made *kings and priests unto God* in this Gospel dispensation *(Revelation 1.6 and 5.10)*. Our role and our witness is to serve as priests in God's temple

---

* *And the Lord spake unto Aaron, saying, Do not drink wine nor strong drink, thou, nor thy sons with thee, when ye go into the tabernacle of the congregation, lest ye die: it shall be a statute for ever throughout your generations: and that ye may put difference between holy and unholy, and between unclean and clean; and that ye may teach the children of Israel all the statutes which the Lord hath spoken unto them by the hand of Moses (Leviticus 10.8-11).* There is a reminder of this law in *Ezekiel 44.21: Neither shall any priest drink wine, when they enter into the inner court.*

‡ *It is not for kings, O Lemuel, it is not for kings to drink wine; nor for princes strong drink: lest they drink, and forget the law, and pervert the judgment of any of the afflicted. Give strong drink unto him that is ready to perish, and wine unto those that be of heavy hearts (Proverbs 31.4-6).*

(which is the church) and to offer up sacrifices of a spiritual nature, namely, our witness to the world.

The apostle Peter describes this witnessing function as a direct counterpart and fulfilment of the Old Testament priesthood. We are, he says, *a spiritual house, an holy priesthood, to offer up spiritual sacrifices . . . a royal priesthood, an holy nation . . . that ye should shew forth the praises of him who hath called you out of darkness into his marvellous light (1 Peter 2.5 and 9).* The present-day church of Christ *is* the temple of Christ. *Hebrews 3.6* confirms this, saying, *whose house are we.*

Many ministers take this parallel very seriously in their own case, believing that *ministers* should not drink, just as priests on duty were not allowed to drink. But surely this does not go far enough, as *all Christians* are members of the priesthood of believers. We are *all* offering up spiritual sacrifices in Christ's temple seven days in every week.

Some may argue that the rule prohibiting alcohol to priests was not meant to be followed literally today, just as the rules of dress for Old Testament priests are not meant to be followed by New Testament 'priests'. But the alcohol ban was given not for ceremonial but for *practical* reasons – and these surely apply today. The priests were not allowed to drink, partly, no doubt, because alcohol had contributed to a great folly being committed in the service of God, but particularly because their minds or moods must not be in the slightest degree impaired for their high and holy tasks, which included the ministry of the Word. This reason is precisely stated in *Leviticus 10.8-11*, with the added warning that death would be the consequence of violation.

Dare we dismiss lightly the conclusion that some obligation rests upon the 'kings and priests' of the New Testament dispensation? Should we scoff so easily at the reasoning of our temperance forebears, and grant ourselves exemption from the very law which God said would be *a statute for ever throughout your generations*?

While in this area of reasoning it is worth noting how these Old Testament requirements bore upon the Lord Jesus Christ. Would He have been liable to observe them? He was, after all, a FAITHFUL *high priest in things pertaining to God (Hebrews 2.17)*. As High Priest, He was (and is) *a minister of the sanctuary, and of the true tabernacle, which the Lord pitched, and not man (Hebrews 8.2).**

Not only was the Lord Jesus Christ the great High Priest over the true tabernacle, but to crown the symbolism, He *was* the true tabernacle. In *John 2.19-21* it is recorded that He said to the Jews, *Destroy this temple, and in three days I will raise it up . . . But he spake of the temple of his body.* Is it conceivable that *such an high*

---

*For the high-priesthood of Christ see also *Hebrews 3.1; 4.14-15; 5.6; 7.26; 10.21.*

priest . . . who is holy, harmless, undefiled (Hebrews 7.26) would have broken His own divine law while officiating on earth as the bodily fulfilment of the earthly Temple? Is it conceivable that the Lord, Who perfectly kept every jot and tittle of the ancient law to fulfil all righteousness, would have done the very thing which He (as the Everlasting Word) had forbidden the earthly priests from doing? Is it conceivable that the King of the Jews and the King of kings would, when He walked on earth, have broken His own law for the *lesser* kings of Old Testament Israel?

The writers of books which advocate the consumption of alcohol in moderation by Christians should be extremely careful before asserting (as they invariably do) that Jesus drank wine.* He may have made it for others at the wedding feast at Cana in Galilee. (The Jews, after all, were still under the Old Testament, which permitted wine in moderation.) He may very well have drunk the fresh fruit of the vine, or the boiled and diluted variety of fermented wine (also called wine) in which the intoxicating properties had been destroyed. But we have no right to say dogmatically that our perfect, law-abiding and great High Priest drank intoxicating wine Himself.

---

* G. I. Williamson, in his book *Wine in the Bible and the Church* (Presbyterian and Reformed, Phillipsburg), says repeatedly, 'Christ did make and use wine.'

SHOULD CHRISTIANS DRINK?

The Lord did indeed say that He came *eating and drinking (Luke 7.34)*; He was contrasting Himself with John the Baptist, whose life of extreme austerity evidently excluded the usual foods and vine-drinks of the people. The Lord's words do not actually indicate that He drank wine in an intoxicating form, however weak.

The Pharisees and lawyers certainly said, *Behold a gluttonous man, and a winebibber, a friend of publicans and sinners,* but that does not prove that the Lord drank alcohol either. The jibe of the Pharisees was as false on the matter of alcohol as it was on the matter of gluttony.

Let us take great care and show all due reverence before we make confident remarks about the Lord Jesus drinking wine. Let us never forget that He fulfilled *all* righteousness in procuring our salvation.

Returning to the teaching that present-day Christians are like priests on duty in the Temple, our argument concludes that God foresaw the emergence of much stronger and more readily available alcoholic drinks, together with the cruel exploitation of alcohol by a world which *lieth in wickedness*, and He therefore built into the ancient priesthood a principle of abstention which in later times would extend to *all* His blood-bought people – the New Testament kingdom of priests.

2. Timothy was Not Alone

OUR SECOND ARGUMENT for the view that Christian abstinence began in the early church is based on the fact that Timothy was an abstainer. In *1 Timothy 5.23*, the words, *Drink no longer water, but use a little wine for thy stomach's sake and thine often infirmities*, obviously indicate that Timothy totally avoided alcohol. The *NASB* reads: *No longer drink water exclusively.* The *NIV* reads: *Stop drinking only water.* Paul was clearly very aware of Timothy's practice.

The significance of this is far greater than is generally appreciated. Timothy, after all, was a most careful imitator of the apostle Paul, and as others have pointed out, it is almost inconceivable that Timothy followed any 'principle' which was not derived from Paul's personal example. After all, it was to Timothy that Paul wrote: *But thou hast fully known my doctrine, manner of life, purpose, faith, longsuffering, charity, patience, persecutions, afflictions (2 Timothy 3.10-11).* The Greek term here translated *fully known,* literally means – *followed closely,* or *conformed to.* The *NKJ* version says: *But you have carefully followed my doctrine, manner of life . . .* The *NASB* says: *But you followed my teaching, conduct . . .* The *Berkley* version says: *But you have adhered to my teaching, my conduct . . .*

The *NIV* follows the *AV* in saying: *You however, know all about my teaching, my way of life,* etc. But the fact that Timothy had closely conformed to all that he saw in Paul is borne out a few sentences later when Paul says: *But as for you, CONTINUE in what you have learned . . . (2 Timothy 3.14, NIV).*

Timothy was an outstanding disciple of Paul. Timothy knew everything about Paul, from the policy and methods of his public work, to his private deportment. He knew also that Paul was intended by God to be an example to all Christian people.

Paul himself frequently appealed to God's people to be imitators of him: in three texts the Greek has *mimics* or close imitators – *1 Corinthians 4.16, 11.1,* and *Philippians 3.17.* He asks that his example be called to mind *in all things (1 Corinthians 11.2).* He asks that the conduct of other teachers be judged according to the *ensample* which he and his immediate helpers, such as

Timothy, provided *(Philippians 3.17)*. The Greek word translated *ensample* in the *AV* means a *die*, or a model or pattern. Paul's ways and lifestyle (reflected in Timothy, Luke, and others) were to be very precisely regarded and followed.

To provide such a pattern was part of the special calling of Paul, as he indicated when he explained to the Thessalonians that he acted in a certain way – *to make ourselves an ensample unto you to follow us (2 Thessalonians 3.9)*. In the light of these texts, the fact of Timothy's abstention from alcohol is a most powerful indication of Paul's own practice.

We note that Paul does not write saying, 'Timothy, you do not have to follow that strange fetish, for there is nothing wrong in wine! Why do you not take wine like the rest of us?' Instead, Paul provides just one reason why Timothy should take wine,[*] and only a little at that.

---

[*] At this point it must be said that we cannot be totally sure that Paul was advocating fermented wine anyway, because the Greek word *oinos* (the most usual NT word for wine) can sometimes mean unfermented grape juice. While in many places in the NT it undoubtedly means fermented wine, it must not be taken for granted that it *always* means this. The word is very plainly used in the Septuagint to cover both fermented and unfermented produce of the vine. It is a broad term, and care is therefore necessary. The fact that Timothy, Paul's close imitator, was an abstainer is certain. What he was to add to his water is not so certain, though for sake of argument we allow that it may have been fermented wine.

That reason is Timothy's susceptibility to stomach troubles and other ailments, presumably aggravated by water or food-borne infection.

The results of modern medical research suggest that if Paul was advocating fermented wine for this purpose, it would ideally have needed to be very weak. In the early 1970s Canadian medical researchers sought to determine the comparative potency of several different beverages against organisms which caused gastro-enteritis. Their results showed fresh orange juice to be most effective, with unfermented grape juice a close second, and fermented wine trailing behind. It was established that grapes contain a substance which is highly effective against stomach organisms, but that this substance is diminished and eventually destroyed by fermentation. In other words, the kind of wine which is marketed today would not have done Timothy's stomach much good at all, but a weaker brew (and the weaker the better) would have given considerable benefit.

There is also very great significance in the fact that Paul mentions Timothy's medicinal requirements in the middle of instructions concerning eldership. From verse 17 (of *1 Timothy 5*) down to verse 25 the subject is the support of elders, their discipline, their unhurried selection, and the evident good conduct shown by suitable candidates . . . Yet before he has finished with these matters, Paul inserts the seemingly misplaced piece of personal advice about alcohol. Unless Paul is being entirely illogical in his sequence of thought, this can only indicate that Timothy's abstention arose from his special office as an elder and a minister of the Word.

Paul had just said – *keep thyself pure.* Was it an essential part of the pure example of such ministers to be abstainers? What made Paul suddenly think of the need to give Timothy an 'exemption' from his policy of rigid abstinence in the middle of a homily on eldership?

The most logical answer is that those early elders and ministers schooled under Paul were all abstainers, and it fell to them to set the example in introducing the standard of the New Testament to the people of God.

It is worth noting also that Paul's list of qualifications for eldership includes (twice) the terse phrase: *Not given to wine* [*] (literally: *not at wine,* or *not beside wine,* or *not lingering at wine*). But as this contrasts sharply with the command to deacons and older women [‡] (where the rule is against *much* wine), it most probably means that elders should not be beside wine at all. If the deacons and older women are permitted *a little,* then the stronger rule for elders must surely mean that they must take none at all.

In summary, we cannot lightly put aside the fact

---

[*] *1 Timothy 3.3; Titus 1.7.*

[‡] *1 Timothy 3.8; Titus 2.3.*

that the abstainer in *1 Timothy 5* was none other than Timothy, the man who followed the apostle Paul *in all things.*

3. The 'Be Sober' and 'Watch' Commands Require Abstention

ANOTHER ARGUMENT that total abstention began in the New Testament (albeit gently, because of the long-established practice of the Jews) is based on the exhortations to sober-mindedness. Many believers today take all these exhortations in a rather general sense, assuming that they merely warn about over-indulgence in alcohol. But abstentionists argue that the strength of the *sober* terms ultimately requires nothing less than total abstention (especially in an age of potent alcoholic drinks).

Take *1 Thessalonians 5.6-8*, where Paul says: *Therefore let us not sleep . . . but let us watch and be SOBER. For they that sleep sleep in the night; and they that be drunken are drunken in the night. But let us, who are of the day, be SOBER.* The word twice translated *sober* indicates – free

71

from intoxicants. It means – to abstain from wine.

Furthermore, the Christian is to *watch*. The Greek here indicates – to keep awake so as to be fully vigilant or alert. Everyone knows that even a small amount of alcohol can make a person a little drowsy. The slowing of a car-driver's reactions as the result of quite modest amounts of alcohol has been repeatedly proved by medical researchers. Alcohol, even in limited amounts, is not conducive to either mental or spiritual alertness, which is the aim of Paul's exhortation.

For good measure this text provides a contrast of lifestyles. On the one hand we see those who are under the power of *this* world – children of the night. They drink. On the other hand, Christians are said to be children of the day; those characterised by freedom from intoxicants and therefore fully alert. This text, taken as a whole, is surely an exhortation to abstinence.

Why do people drink the wines and other alcoholic drinks of today? Is it purely for the taste, or is it not also for the sense, however slight, of relaxation or well-being which the drink provides? Is it to be 'warmed up inside' on a cold day, or 'a little cheered' on a dull one? Is it to 'brighten' a meal? Modern alcoholic drinks undoubtedly affect the mind and mood, even when taken in moderate amounts. An intoxicating drug is absorbed into the body which immediately suppresses the higher faculties, acting in direct opposition to all the New Testament exhortations to soberness, wakefulness and vigilance. Whatever people may claim, only two glasses of most undiluted, present-day wines are sufficient to bring their personality and senses under the power of alcohol to a perceptible degree.

Consider *Titus 2.2*, where Paul instructs that *the aged men be sober, grave, temperate.* Once again the word *sober* means free from intoxicants, but how free? Let the context decide! The passage lays down the ideal for elderly believers, those who have proved the Lord over many years, and who provide an example of faith, character and wisdom to younger believers. These are to be *grave* which means venerable, or worthy of utmost respect. *Temperate* means safe or sound in mind. They are to be acute, sagacious, wise, dependable, and absolutely safe in mental judgement.

The word *sober,* in this context, does not merely mean that the older men are not to become tipsy. It means that intoxicants must never be allowed to cloud their judgement and slow their minds. It is the glory of older saints to be bright and crystal clear in their minds, possessing the sharp faculties of those who have grown in grace to be 'princes with God'.

1 Peter 1.13 places *sober* in the context of girding up the loins of the mind! To Peter, being sober was a condition which allowed the mind to function at its very best. In other words, it implied total abstention from intoxicants. In *1 Peter 4.7 sober* is put in the context of watching unto prayer, the highest activity of the clear mind. In *1 Peter 5.8* the word *sober* is put in the context of watching out for our adversary the devil, who walks about as a roaring lion *seeking whom he may devour.*

If we were to explore all the exhortations to be 'safe-minded' (another Greek word often translated as *sober*), we would see yet another family of texts which rule out any intoxicating interference with our most precious human faculty – the mind.

A final text lending weight to this particular argument is *Ephesians 5.15: See then that ye walk circumspectly.* The Greek word translated *circumspectly* means *most exactly;* extremely precisely; accurately. The Christian life is compared to a task or a craft which needs such precision that there is no room for the slightest deviation or mistake. A tremor of the hand will ruin the work. As believers, our minds, moods and spirits must never be blurred or befuddled, not even to the smallest degree. The very nature of the Christian life demands that our mental acumen is never influenced, dampened or retarded to any degree by the powerful alcoholic drugs of this world.

We do accept that in Bible times those believers who had always used in moderation the weak alcohol of Israelite culture were not immediately pressed to abandon it. But the new standard was nevertheless proclaimed as the proper ideal, and exemplified in the lives of the Lord's messengers. That, according to abstentionists, is the force of the texts just reviewed.

4. The Duty of Example

THE ARGUMENT that we must be abstainers out of consideration for younger or weaker believers, and for people vulnerable to alcoholism, is the only abstention argument which some anti-abstinence Christian writers seem to be aware of, and they attack it with great vigour. It is often based on such texts as *Romans 14.15* and *21*, which contain the words: *Destroy not him with thy meat, for whom Christ died . . . It is good neither to eat flesh, nor to drink wine, nor any thing whereby thy brother stumbleth, or is offended, or is made weak.*

The argument is that a Christian who drinks in moderation may lead another, perhaps younger Christian, to follow suit. If the other person then finds the attraction of alcohol too great to resist, and falls into sin, perhaps even into alcoholism, then a burden of responsibility rests with the one who set a dangerous example in the first place. It is argued that Christian compassion and responsibility unite to say that we should abstain from alcohol to prevent this kind of tragedy.

The opponents of abstention have a field-day with this argument, leaping to point out that the text is taken out of context by abstainers. As our footnote shows,* they are correct in this charge. Paul's words do not, when correctly interpreted, speak about setting a bad example.

---

* When Paul spoke of the *weaker brother* (the one likely to stumble), he was not thinking of a person who might be led to take up drink, and so experience a sad fall. He actually had in mind a brother who was weak because he believed that if he ate or drank certain things he would somehow be defiled and made unclean in God's sight. Such superstitious fetishes were apparently prevalent among Christians who had been saved from religious backgrounds which taught such ideas. Paul taught that *the kingdom of God is not meat and drink*, and that *all things indeed are pure.* In other words, no ordinary, wholesome food substance or drink should be regarded as intrinsically evil or defiling to the soul. If a young and 'weak' Christian, fearful of eating or drinking the wrong thing, was led into doing so, he would obviously feel that he had sinned grievously, and suffer torment of conscience. Nevertheless, Paul insists on gentleness and kindness toward the 'weaker brother', presumably so that he may have time to grow out of his over-scrupulous ideas without hurt to his conscience. It is true, therefore, that this text is not really an appropriate one for pressing the point which we abstainers are making.

However, the principle which abstainers act on – that a bad example may cause many Christians (and unbelievers also) to succumb to alcohol – is a sound one which is taught throughout the New Testament. We cannot understand why pro-alcohol writers should think that they have answered this point merely by pointing out that *one* text is inappropriately used.

What about all the other texts which command believers not to set a potentially injurious example to their fellows? We find such a text, for example, in *2 Corinthians 6.3-4*, where Paul writes: *Giving no offence in any thing, that the ministry be not blamed: but in all things approving ourselves as the ministers of God.* Paul then adds that we do this *by kindness . . . by love unfeigned.* Among other things this means that we must never adopt unnecessary habits which could lead others into disaster, and discredit the Gospel ministry. Our example must be characterised by *kindness.*

2 Corinthians 11.29 is a verse which reveals Paul's tender concern for the casualties among the people of God: *Who is weak, and I am not weak? who is offended, and I burn not?* The *NASB* renders the last part of this verse in this way: *Who is led into sin without my intense concern?* Paul, our example, avoids anything which may cause another to stumble into sin. We recognise that in this present age of strong and abundant alcoholic drinks, coupled with the social pressures of a godless generation, there will be vulnerable Christians – perhaps we ourselves! We *must* have intense concern about the possible consequences of young people being led into the use of alcohol.

Some anti-abstinence writers reveal a rather startling lack of compassion for people who might be especially susceptible to alcohol. G. I. Williamson, for example, following J. G. Vos, vehemently denies that some people are more susceptible to alcohol than others. He is outraged at the idea that some people could turn out to be *constitutional* alcoholics.

Mr Williamson thinks that this is the same as saying that some people are constitutional homosexuals. Worse, he thinks that the very idea makes God the author of sin, because it charges Him with creating some people with a special susceptibility to drunkenness.

As far as G. I. Williamson is concerned, people who fall into the clutches of alcohol have only themselves to blame, and therefore no righteous person need abstain from alcohol for fear of setting a dangerous example. We believe this to be very weak reasoning, and that it also exhibits indifference to the suffering of alcohol victims. While we agree that excessive drinking is a sin, and that human beings are personally responsible and accountable to God for all sins, it is nevertheless futile to deny that alcohol is a drug which affects many people in a particularly drastic way.

Susceptible people metabolise alcohol in such a way that they have a much greater tendency to become dependent upon it. This is a fact now well established and documented by medical researchers the world over, some of whom now believe they have identified the physiological cause of this special susceptibility to alcohol. It is also well attested that women are susceptible to alcohol at lower levels than men, and that they are more liable to suffer other alcohol-related health damage.

In a world full of strong alcoholic drinks, Christian compassion requires that we take very seriously the special vulnerability of numerous people. And we do well to remember that this vulnerability relates not only to full-scale alcoholism, but also to the mood changes induced by quite low intakes of alcohol. Without doubt, some people *are* more susceptible than others, and Christians who drink *are* responsible for the damage which their example may bring about in other lives. With or without the *Romans 14* passage, it is a New Testament Christian duty to scrupulously avoid leading others into sin, and into activities which lead to spiritual harm.

Kenneth Gentry, in his book *The Christian and Alcoholic Beverages* (which argues in favour of drinking wine in moderation) uses the following argument to suggest that no one is potentially susceptible to alcohol – 'The assertion that the imbibing of alcohol is a form of reckless conduct in the light of the many unknown "potential alcoholics" impugns the character of both the apostles and even the Lord Jesus Christ Himself. Did not they partake of wine openly (eg: *Luke 7.33-35*)? Did Jesus not know of "potential alcoholics" or of "constitutional alcoholics"?'

Our reply to this line of reasoning is to point out once again that the normal beverage wine of Palestine in those days was very much weaker than the table wines, fortified wines and spirits of later ages, and there was no risk whatsoever of alcohol-dependency or alcoholism being triggered unless a drinker went a *very long way* beyond the ordinary levels of consumption.

Today, however, our culture is different, and large quantities of beers, wines and spirits are aggressively pressed upon the rising generation. Only two glasses of a strong modern wine may have an immediate effect upon a vulnerable drinker.

We must recognise that some sins, once launched into, may to a great extent 'take over' the lives of those who indulge in them. We therefore protect the young, not only from evil substances such as narcotic drugs, but also from the most subtle drug of all – alcohol. Without doubt this is the pre-eminent drug among young people at the present time.

Marijuana, cannabis, heroin, acid (LSD), crack and other hallucinatory or euphoric drugs abound, but chief among all psycho-active substances for the overwhelming majority of teenagers is alcohol, which has the advantage of being the easiest drug to obtain, and the one which meets with the approval of adult society, including many Christians.

In *ABC of Alcohol*, a collection of articles by leading UK specialists in alcoholism (published by the *British Medical Journal*), Doctors A. Paton and J. F. Porter point out that the age at which drinking begins has fallen to between 12 and 14 years. Furthermore, a survey of young men between 18 and 24 showed that 18% were already heavy drinkers (ie: drinking more than 80gm of alcohol per day, or ten glasses of wine, or five pints of beer).

Writers who are opposed to abstention should not lightly throw aside the burden of example to the young. If we appear to approve of today's alcoholic drinks, we will certainly lower the guard of younger people around us, and in so doing we may contribute to someone's future tragic experience. This, we assert, is a heavy responsibility.

5. Wine is a New Testament Symbol for Evil

YET ANOTHER ARGUMENT in support of abstinence having been introduced in New Testament times is derived from the fact that wine is used as a symbol of evil in the last book of the Bible. While in the Old Testament wine was often a symbol of a successful harvest and prosperity (eg: *Psalm 104.14-15* and *Proverbs 3.10*), in the New Testament wine is used as a symbol of wrath, judgement, and also of human evil.* It is as though the Bible anticipates the inevitable decline of wine over the course of history from the category of 'things acceptable' to that of 'evil and harmful'.

---

* We are not including here the use of the vine plant as a representation of the Lord and His people.

Revelation 14.8 speaks of how fallen Babylon *made all nations drink of the wine of the wrath of her fornication.* The *NASB* reads: *The wine of the passion of her immorality.* Wine provides a most suitable picture for something which appears to be attractive, but which by steady enticement draws the person into an inflamed and lawless condition.

Revelation 14.10 speaks of *the wine of the wrath of God.* Most commentators say that freshly trodden grapes here picture the 'blood' of judgement. Wine again pictures the fierceness of God's wrath in *Revelation 16.19*, and the fornication of the *great whore* in *Revelation 17.2* and *18.3.* In *Revelation 18.13* wine is listed among things which symbolise the excessive indulgence and luxury of a wicked world system which captures the souls of men. In *Revelation 6.6* it probably stands as the drink of the wicked rich in a world of inequality (though this is open to debate).

The point is that by the final book of the Bible, wine had become a regular symbol of the enticements of evil and its just punishment. This certainly shows that the apostle John had no high regard for wine, and more importantly, that the conscience of the early church was being trained to take a new, low view of alcoholic beverages.

6. There is no 'Wine' in the Lord's Supper

ANOTHER ARGUMENT in favour of abstinence having begun in the New Testament is derived from the accounts of the institution of the Lord's Supper. To begin with, it is surely highly significant that no formal wine word is employed in any of the accounts of the Lord's Supper, either in the four Gospels, or in *1 Corinthians 11*. Throughout these accounts the term *cup* is used, the liquid within being called *this fruit of the vine (Matthew 26.29)*.

What kind of wine was employed for this Supper? Was it a watered-down wine typical of the ancient passover feast? Or was it wine which had been boiled and diluted, thus losing all potency? Alternatively, was it unfermented grape juice? The very least we must say is that no one can be absolutely certain what kind of vine produce was in the cup of the Lord. We repeat, there-fore, that it is wrong, presumptuous and even foolish to say *dogmatically*, as some pro-wine authors do, that the Lord both drank and gave alcoholic wine at the institu-tion of the Lord's Supper.

We can, however, make suggestions about the nature of the wine at the Lord's Supper by considering the new significance of wine as a symbol. Matthew, Mark and Luke give an almost identical record of the precise words which the Lord Jesus used, and these have immense significance. First Jesus took bread, broke it, and gave it to the disciples, saying, *Take, eat: this is my body*. After this He took the cup, gave thanks, and distributed it to them. Then the Lord said these words: *This is my blood of the new testament, which is shed for many (Mark 14.24).*

It is particularly important to note the use of the word *new*. The blood of Christ is the efficacy, sign and seal of a *new* testament. The word *new* in the Greek is *kainos*, which means new in *character* (ie: different). The new testament was new in the sense that it was entirely new in character, and different from the old testament. (The Greek has another word – *neos* – to describe things that are new only in the sense of being young.)

What kind of wine would be a fitting symbol of a new and different testament? The argument used by many Christian abstainers is this – it would be a *different* wine. The old passover feast, symbolising the *old* testament, was usually kept with diluted, fermented wine, but in the *new* feast – the Lord's Supper – the wine has a new and a different symbolic role. It would in future stand for the blood of the *new* (different) testament. Therefore it would be a *new* (different) wine. It would not be like the traditional cup of the old passover ceremony. (Nor would it be like the wine by which a godless world would be increasingly dominated.) A *new* testament and a *new* feast in a *new* church calls for a *new* (a different) cup.

The Jews in their passover feast ate unleavened bread, or 'uncorrupted' bread as a symbol of purity. They distributed four cups of wine in thankfulness for the successful harvest and the provision of the vine. However, in the Lord's Supper the cup has an altogether different significance. It now represents the precious blood of the Lamb of God once slain – the pure, holy, spotless Lamb. The Jews of old had unleavened bread as a symbol of purity; the new cup of the Lord's Supper calls for 'unleavened' or unfermented wine as the only fitting symbol of the blood of the perfect and righteous Son of God.

When the Lord Jesus bore away the sins of His people on Calvary's cross He bore the wrath of God. His sacred body was punished for us, and trodden down as *the winepress of the fierceness and wrath of Almighty God* upon our sins. The biblical picture is of the blood of grapes *freshly pressed*, and therefore the appropriate

87

symbol of the shed blood of Christ is the fresh, unfermented blood of the grape.

Such observations as these have led many to the view
that at the inauguration of the Lord's Supper our Lord
brought in a *new* cup, departing from previous Jewish
custom. Untainted, unfermented wine was introduced,
representing the newness, difference and purity of the
new testament, and the blood of that testament.

A difficulty with this assumption is the issue of the
availability of unfermented grape juice, other than
during the months of the grape harvest. It is widely
assumed today that in the first century AD there was no
effective method of preserving grape juice, which begins
to ferment by itself as soon as it is left to stand.

The present writer can offer no solution to this problem. It may be that we underestimate the know-how of
those days. Or it may be that a fermented wine boiled to
dispose of the alcohol and then diluted (the well-known
beverage described earlier), represented the unfermented product of the vine outside the season when
fresh grape juice was available. Certainly, our understanding of passages of Scripture should not be
determined by our imperfect historical knowledge of
Bible times, and the possibility that a *different* wine is
implied in the Lord's Supper texts is richly consistent
with the symbolism of the Supper.

The remark has often been made that the Lord's
Supper of the early church must have involved

fermented wine because people at Corinth became drunk at the Table. But the occurrence of drunkenness was the result of the Corinthians gathering for a normal meal at the same time that the Lord's Supper was held. This is made very clear in *1 Corinthians 11.21*. In the event Paul tells them to eat at home if they cannot share this ordinary meal in a proper manner. The Lord's Supper is thus shown to be something quite distinct from their ordinary eating, in which some, if not many, people were clearly still drinking wine. (We remember that the new ideal of abstinence was introduced in a gentle way.)

To abstentionists, the new and different nature of the cup also bears testimony to the perfect ways of the Lord, Who knows all things, and Who would not have His people sanctifying and approving an industry whose wickedness and guilt would only increase as the centuries passed.

Conclusion –
An Unhallowed Thirst?

IN THESE PAGES we have sought to show that alcoholic drinks have dramatically changed since Bible times, and that they now fall foul of the standards laid down by Christ for His people. We have also pointed to the evidence for the introduction of abstention during New Testament times.

The Temperance Movement of 170 years ago was a truly Christian reaction to the tragedy of nineteenth-century drunkenness and alcohol-related misery. Countless Christian hearts could not bear it, and did their utmost to rescue men, women and children from physical and spiritual disaster, dissociating themselves personally from the 'demon drink'.

Today, strangely, there is a new and widespread ignorance about the influence of 'modern' alcoholic drinks on human faculties of mind and co-ordination. Medical writers on this subject agree that changes occur within thirty minutes of a first drink – changes not discerned by drinkers, but detectable by proficiency tests, which reveal clearly deteriorating responses in judgement. Driving skill, for example, is certainly affected by even two glasses of wine, while after three, drinkers themselves begin to feel carefree and liberated from their anxieties and inhibitions.

Alcohol – Our Favourite Drug (the 1986, 213-page report by leading medical specialists in alcohol-related problems) puts it in this way:–

'After a few drinks conversation appears to sparkle, dull people seem more interesting, and feeble jokes funny . . . the disinhibiting effects of alcohol may release suppressed feelings of aggression and hostility . . . Focusing and the ability to follow objects with the eyes are greatly impaired even by low doses of alcohol . . . Moderate or even small doses of alcohol may substantially impair performance on standard intellectual tests. Memory for words, fluency in their use, and the quality of word association are all impaired . . . Drinkers break into their partner's conversation more frequently, and their responses show less knowledge of what their partners are talking about . . . Fine tests of discrimination, or memory, and of arithmetical ability show that impairment begins at low blood-alcohol levels . . . Unfortunately, many people under the influence of alcohol believe that their performance is normal, or even improved.'

Again we repeat the questions which arise from *1 Corinthians 6.12* and *10.23* – Is it expedient (fitting or appropriate)? Does it bring me under its power? Does it edify? And the questions arising from *Philippians 4.8* – Is it honest, and just, and pure, and lovely, and of good report, and virtuous, and worthy of praise – even in moderation?

The secular physicians in the report just referred to do not write as abolitionists or total abstainers, but as medical professionals who want to see a powerful psycho-active drug recognised for what it is. They conclude: 'Our society has chosen to co-exist with a potentially dangerous and addictive drug. Society should, though, be appalled by the present state of affairs and entirely unwilling to witness continued loss and suffering of this order.'

We ask yet again, Which side is alcohol now on? Which category is it in? Where would the Lord have us, His people, stand in relation to an industry which is the world's largest producer of an intoxicating substance? Should Christians drink today? We believe the answer is resoundingly clear!

Appendix 1
The Wine Words of the Old Testament

THE FOUR HEBREW words which refer to drink made from grapes or other fruits are – *yayin, tirosh, shekar* and *'asis.*

Yayin, is used 141 times, and judging from the context in which it is used, it refers to fermented grape wine. It is the wine which made Noah and Lot drunk *(Genesis 9.21 and 19.32-5).* We have already shown that the common wine of those days was very weak (and probably also diluted with water before drinking), though even the weakest, drunk undiluted and in quantity, was intoxicating. Stronger 'brews' could no doubt be made (probably 8%–10%) by those who wanted them, and particularly by those who sought a more intoxicating effect.

However, we must not forget that *yayin,* as a term,

would include any drink *derived* from fermented wine, so that boiled and freshly diluted wine-cordial (shorn of its alcoholic content) would also be called *yayin.*

Yayin – fermented wine – was to be included in the offerings made to God, and was wholly approved (along with *shekar,* or 'strong drink') in *Deuteronomy 14.23* and *26.* This last verse referred to is worth examining, as too much is read into it by writers who are against abstention.

Moses here says: *And thou shalt bestow that money for whatsoever thy soul lusteth after, for oxen, or for sheep, or for wine, or for strong drink, or for whatsoever thy soul desireth: and thou shalt eat there before the Lord thy God, and thou shalt rejoice, thou, and thine household.*

This verse is constantly quoted as the Lord's justification of fermented wine, together with the stronger drinks derived in those days from other fruits (eg: date wine and barley beer). However, neither the offerings, nor this verse, throw any light on what the Israelites actually did with the wines. Fermented wine was certainly approved for them, but how strong was it, and in the case of the 'strong drink', how did they use it? The range of uses would (as we show in this book) include cooking, drinking in diluted form, and even boiling prior to dilution to make a non-alcoholic cordial. Moses does not say anything about the *use* of wine.

We note that *Deuteronomy 14.26* does not mention what precisely is to be done with oxen or sheep, it simply says that they may be bought and eaten. It would, of course, be foolish to take the verse as an approval of raw meat, or an approval of the blood (elsewhere forbidden), and so on. The verse assumes that much will be done to the meat before consumption, and the same allowance should be extended to the *yayin* and *shekar*.

Tirosh, which is used 38 times in the Old Testament, refers to the 'must', or the fresh, new wine, which has undergone only aerobic, and not anaerobic, fermentation. Like *yayin*, references show it to be intoxicating, but being so new it was probably the weakest wine of all.

'Asis, used only five times, is another wine word. It means 'pressed', and most probably refers to unfermented, fresh grape juice. Two references *(Joel 1.5* and *Isaiah 49.26)* use this word to denote intoxicating wine, but the verses are poetic and probably point to the innocence of the original product, which became an offensive substance once it was fermented and applied to the ultimate goal of drunkenness.

Shekar (translated 'strong drink' in the *AV*) is plainly an intoxicating, fermented wine, the word *shekar* probably suggesting that it was stronger than the grape wine of the day. In 21 out of 22 occurrences of this word it is used alongside *yayin* (the grape wine), implying that it refers to wines derived from other fruits.

Shekar meets with much condemnation in the Old Testament (probably because of its greater strength). It appears as an approved substance in the offerings, and in *Deuteronomy 14* (a fact already discussed).

To summarise, apart from the little used word *'asis,* the wine words of the Old Testament all indicate a fermented product, but could include diluted or boiled (non-alcoholic) servings. It would be foolish to insist that the wine could not intoxicate, but it is equally misguided to imagine that a strong product, akin to present-day wine, was the common beverage of those days. *Shekar,* the strongest, could not (scientifically) have exceeded 14%, and probably, in practice, not more than 10%, given the poor technology of the time, and *shekar* chiefly meets with disapproval in the Old Testament.

Appendix 2
The Mixed Wine of
Isaiah 1.22

WRITERS WHO ARE OPPOSED to abstention cast doubt on the probability that the Israelites mixed their wine with water (in common with the Greeks and the Romans) by appealing to *Isaiah 1.21-22*, where the addition of water to wine is referred to as a shameful thing. In this passage the prophet denounces Jerusalem, saying, *How is the faithful city become an harlot! it was full of judgment; righteousness lodged in it; but now murderers. Thy silver is become dross, thy wine mixed with water.*

Certainly, the weakening or mutilation of the wine with water is here rebuked as a fraudulent, sinful act (in parallel with the addition of dross to the silver coinage). Whether these crimes were literally committed, or whether they are poetic figures of spiritual hypocrisy, the fact remains that the adulteration of the wine with water is condemned.

But this proves nothing, because the prophet is speaking in these verses of sins which were committed *secretly* and *fraudulently*. He is speaking about acts surrounded by deceit and unfaithfulness (such as acts of marital unfaithfulness). Normally when wine was diluted in the ancient world, it was mixed with water immediately before serving, in full view of the partakers. There was no deceit or fraud about it. The deceitful act described by Isaiah can only refer to a watering of the wine in storage, or before sale. Thus the strictures of Isaiah have no bearing whatsoever on whether or not the Israelites diluted their wine on serving.

Appendix 3
Strengths of Modern Beers, Wines and Spirits

	% alcohol	calories
Beers (per half-pint)		
Lager	3 - 7	80 - 200
Ale	3 - 7	60 - 400
Stout	4 - 8	150 - 200
Table Wines (per small glass)		
Red	8 - 14	80 - 95
White & Rosé	8 - 14	75 - 90
Sparkling	12	90
(Champagne)		

SHOULD CHRISTIANS DRINK?

	% alcohol	calories
Dessert & cocktail wines (per small glass)		
Sherry & Madeira	15 - 20	65 - 75
Port	15 - 20	165
Vermouth	15 - 20	80
Spirits (per single measure)		
Brandy	40	75
Whisky	37 - 40	58
Rum	40	55
Gin	37 - 40	55
Vodka	37.5	55
Liqueurs (per single measure)		
	22 - 55	80

Appendix 4
Texts that Suggest God Approves of the Inebriating Effects of Wine

BIBLE READERS are sometimes perplexed by a few verses which appear superficially to condone a very mild degree of intoxication, or a 'merry' condition, brought about by wine. Some anti-abstention writers lay great emphasis upon these verses, claiming that happy sensations arising from the drinking of wine are approved by the Lord.

Psalm 104.14-15 is the most-quoted text. It reads: *He causeth the grass to grow for the cattle, and herb for the service of man: that he may bring forth food out of the earth; and wine that maketh glad the heart of man, and oil to make his face to shine, and bread which strengtheneth man's heart.*

Kenneth L. Gentry in *The Christian and Alcoholic Beverages* says: 'A moderate gladdening of the heart was not forbidden, according to this and other scriptures (cf *2 Samuel 13.28; Esther 1.10; Ecclesiastes 9.7* and *10.19; Zechariah 9.15* and *10.7*).' This is an astonishing point of view which, we shall show, finds no support in the texts cited.

It should be obvious that *Psalm 104.14-15* does not speak of the literal effects of the vine, oil and grain crops on the *bodies* of people, but the effects on their *emotions* as they gathered a bounteous harvest. The grain gave them confidence for the survival and well-being of their families. The oil assured them of a 'civilised' existence, enhancing their cooking techniques, enabling them to make refined foodstuffs, lighting the evening lamps, and providing healing ointments. The vine gave special pleasure, bringing a sweet, enjoyable, sanitary wine into their homes throughout the year.

The psalmist speaks of the happiness, anticipation and confidence which arose from the harvesting and possessing of these good things, and not of their literal, physiological effects upon the bodies of the people.

2 Samuel 13.28 and *Esther 1.10* (cited by Kenneth Gentry) merely record the drunken behaviour of the immoral Amnon, and of the arrogant Persian king, Ahasuerus. They certainly do not condone the intoxicating effects of alcohol!

Ecclesiastes 9.7 reads: *Go thy way, eat thy bread with*

joy, and drink thy wine with a merry heart. We must first point out that no degree of intoxication, however slight, is necessarily implied in this verse. The basic thought is that people must have a grateful, appreciative attitude to the benefits of life. (The passage goes on to say, in graphic language, that life should be like a thanksgiving service all the time!)

However, it is most probable that Solomon's exhortation is cynical in tone. He is saying, in effect, 'You unbelievers had better learn to enjoy every benefit that you have while you are alive, because you will soon forfeit them all – *in the grave, whither thou goest.*'

Either way, it is quite wrong to use this passage as an authorisation for believers to drink wine so that it affects their mood.

Ecclesiastes 10.19 gives this observation: *A feast is made for laughter, and wine maketh merry: but money answereth all things.* Drinking to achieve some level of intoxication is undoubtedly in mind in this verse, but does it meet with God's approval?

Solomon's point is that feasting and drinking have no power to get anything done, or to solve problems (by contrast with the deployment of money). They may take people's minds off their problems, but that is all.

Another interpretation suggests that Solomon criticises all who look to feasts, drinking *and* money for their security and fulfilment, rather than looking to God. Again, whichever view one takes of the text, it certainly offers no approval of intoxication, however mild.

Zechariah 9.15 is part of a prophecy telling how the Jews would rise up victoriously against the Greeks in the Maccabean era (the second century BC). Zechariah says that they will *make a noise as through wine* (or be boisterous as through wine). Does this statement sanction the use of wine to produce 'gladdening of heart'?

The fact is that Zechariah visualises the conquering Jews 'under the image of a lion, who devours his enemy and then treads them underfoot' (Moore). Moreover, it is this lion who is intoxicated with the blood of his enemies, as with wine!

Would the Jews literally eat the Greeks, or tread them underfoot? Of course not! All the statements are graphic images. The lion, roaring as if intoxicated by the blood of his victims, illustrates the confidence and determination which God would give to a previously demoralised Jewish people. There is no question of *literal* intoxication being sanctioned by God for His people in this text.

In *Zechariah 10.7* the prophet predicts that the heart of Ephraim *shall rejoice as through wine.* This great joy will come to them either at the coming of the Messiah, or at some yet future restoration of the Jews. Once again, the prophet does not say that Ephraim would literally be intoxicated, but that they (or a representative remnant of them) would experience a degree of pleasure which could only be paralleled, in human terms, by intoxication. We see the point, of course, in *Acts 2.13* where scornful onlookers said of the disciples as they joyfully preached the wonderful works of God in the languages of all the people: *These men are full of new wine.*

Anti-abstention writers search in vain for a single Scripture text which gives God's approval for the use of wine to produce a 'happy' or intoxicated condition. The weak and diluted wines of the Jews did not produce even mild intoxication unless drunk to great excess.

Bibliography

Adkins, Jan, 1971, *The Craft of Winemaking*, Walker Publishing, New York.

Bustanoby, Andre S., 1987, *The Wrath of Grapes, Drinking and the Church Divided*, Baker Book House, Grand Rapids.

Douglas, George C.M., *Wine*, in the *Imperial Bible Dictionary*, Vol 6, Blackie & Son, London.

Gentry, Kenneth L., 1986, *The Christian and Alcoholic Beverages, A Biblical Perspective*, Baker Book House, Grand Rapids.

Hyams, Edward, 1987, *Dionysus: A Social History of the Wine Vine*, Sidgwick & Jackson, London.

Jennings, Isaac, 1870, *Wine — A Cyclopædia of Biblical Literature*, (Kitto), Vol 3, Adam and Charles Black, Edinburgh.

Paton, Alex (Ed.), 1988, *ABC of Alcohol*, British Medical Journal, London.

Robinson, Jancis, 1988, *The Demon Drink: A User's Guide*, Methuen, London.

Royal College of Psychiatrists Special Committee, 1986, *Alcohol – Our Favourite Drug*, Tavistock Publications, London.

Williamson, G. I., 1976, *Wine in the Bible and the Church*, Presbyterian and Reformed Publishing Company, Phillipsburg.